His

Grace & Mercy

S.K. Edwards

Choice Publishing Inc.

Presents

His
Grace & Mercy

By S.K. Edwards

S.K. Edwards

Copyright 2012 by

S.K. Edwards

All rights reserved, including the right to reproduce this book or portions thereof in any form whatsoever, without the written permission of the author.

Unless otherwise noted, all Scripture quotations are from the New King James Version, and New Living Version of the Bible.

His Grace & Mercy

Dedication

S.K. Edwards

I Almost Let Go

My younger sister, Cheryl Sonya "Chu Chu" Edwards, was brutally killed inside of a Dollar Store on her day off. She had just gotten home after finishing her shift for the Richmond city police department as a school crossing guard. She had just settled in when the manager of her part time job called and informed her that they were short staffed and asked if she could come in. She needed the extra money so she agreed. Well, according to police, someone robbed the store after it had closed. Forensics showed that she was stocking the shelves, and must have heard a commotion, and went to investigate. Apparently she walked in on the manager being killed, so she, too, was brutally murdered.

My sister was a beautiful person. She never drank, smoked, did drugs, went to clubs or anything. An outing to her was taking my grandmother to yard sales on Saturday or in church all day Sunday.

His Grace & Mercy

When she was taken away from me, my world collapsed. This was my best friend. We shared everything. I was lost and didn't think I could go on. I was told that hell would be the worst feeling anyone will have, so I knew I was in hell. I let go; at least I thought I did.

That's until, one day, I heard this song by Kurt Karr, called I almost let go. This song saved me. God gave it to me at the right time. The power in the words to this song will grab you So as I dedicate this book to my sister, and I dedicate this song to you on her behalf. I would like to I hope that they both bring you what you need understand His Grace & Mercy!!!

S.K. Edwards

I would also like to dedicate this book to the Late Bishop James F. Brown. To grow up under the teachings of this man is a privilege that I wish everyone could have experienced. Remembering his strong presence in that pulpit, the patience, the understanding, made me the man I am today.

His legacy is carried on through the strength of his beautiful wife, Chief Apostle Olive C. Brown, and his sons Bishop Joel Brown, Bishop Rudy brown Jr., and Bishop Marvin Brown. A conversation with this family will definitely help you understand His Grace & Mercy!!!

His Grace & Mercy

Contents

The Bible 11

The Change 15

The Wrong Hands 27

The Battle Within 33

Prayer 51

The Big Con 73

Denial 79

Favor 85

Soar 93

One More Move 103

Praise 107

Assist 119

Bad 123

Testimonies 125

Calendar Quotes 137

S.K. Edwards

His Grace & Mercy

Have you ever wondered how you could pick up all the pieces of your broken life? Have you ever awakened in the middle of the night and had a word from heaven burning in your spirit? Have you ever stood on the word of God and seen your situation turn in your favor? Have you ever fought your way to church and it seemed like you couldn't get there fast enough? Have you ever just gone before God with nothing but thanksgiving as your praise? I got it. Maybe you doubted God, because you felt like your prayer was unheard and at that moment a miracle happened in your life? Have you ever wondered how it would be to just walk around heaven all day? Maybe you've wondered if your nearly departed really found each other in Glory. Have you ever belted praise to God from the very bottom of your heart that was the very example of a Hallelujah moment? Have you ever looked back at your situation and realized that you had just made it through? Despite all these questions I want you to be proud of yourselves, because you obviously realize that there is a God. Realizing that he is mighty and able to deliver you will bring you to these questions, carry you through, and reward you on the other side. This is all possible because you believe. This is where you experience the presence of God in your life. The life that you are living is never the same from that moment forth. This happens for some people right at the altar on any given Wednesday or Sunday, or maybe even Saturday. The point is that it happened. You can't go back at this point. You are the "super hero" in your life. You are a hero because you came out of some bad situation or broken circumstance. I hope that you understand your super ability, or abilities are best and most effective when used on someone else other than yourself. The confirmation of God's covering is very evident at this point. Make sure that the people who are around you in your tight knit circle have a revelation of who you are. The sooner they and you realize that a change has begun in your life, the easier it will be to adjust to the change. We all should want to be at this point sooner or later. This climax in your life is a result of your perseverance. Don't let anybody or anything turn you around. Keep yourself focused and fixed on your transformation. Let all the people around you adjust in their own way, whether it be staying in your life or choosing to break off ties with you. Show them that you are under construction by your actions. We are capable of building people up and empowering these same people when our walk is similar to our talk. Build people up with the word of God and reinforce that with positivity. The awesome part is that some lives have already been built and only require maintenance. Great are the tender mercies of our Lord of Lords. We are always provided with what we need all around us. Hallelujah. This is where the issues of your heart turn into gratefulness and praise.

S.K. Edwards

Let Christ Shine Through

His Grace & Mercy

The Bible

S.K. Edwards

By definition the Bible is *The sacred book of Christianity, a collection of ancient writings including the books of both the Old Testament and the New Testament.*

Actually the bible was written to guide us through life. Everything that we need, and will see during our lifetime is in the bible. As a matter of fact, the bible stands for, **B**asic **I**nstructions **B**efore **L**eaving **E**arth. *Ecclesiastes 6:12 says, "For who knows what is good for a person in life, during the few and meaningless days they pass through like a shadow."*

Even though the bible is interpreted differently by many religions, the concept is the same. But as humans we have a tendency to question things that we have no control over. So when we hear have faith and believe, our carnal mind wants us to ask why. You don't need to ask why. Did God ask why should he send his only begotten son to suffer for our sins so that we wouldn't have to? Did God ask why

His Grace & Mercy

should he wake you up this morning? Did God ask should he give you another chance every time you mess up? If you want to ask why, ask why about that.

Well I believe we all were appointed a guardian angel to help guide our steps, at the same time, give us free will to make our own choices. We don't always make wise choices so, when we fall, know that his "Grace and Mercy" is there to catch you. Now that's not saying that you won't be held accountable for your actions, but can be forgiven.

If you believe in the bible and the words it speaks, you can't go wrong.

S.K. Edwards

If you ask he will forgive

His Grace & Mercy

THE CHANGE

Galatians 5: 1

Stand fast therefore in the liberty wherewith Christ hath made us free, and be not entangled again with the yoke of bondage.

The yokes of bondage are the things that have previously or currently are stopping you from making the changes necessary in your life. Galatians 5: 10 reads;"I have confidence in you through the Lord, that ye will be none otherwise minded: but he that troubleth you shall bear his judgment, whosoever he be." This is or should be all the comfort that you need. I am in no way saying that this will be easy but it shouldn't be hard, if you truly are seeking change. I believe that you will already know what adjustments are needed. The people that are fixed in your life will remain in place. The people in your life that were only seasonal will do what seasons do. This is where you get the term, "fair weather friends", from. This is actually a pretty good one to hold on to and add to your mental rolodex. This term is the perfect way to explain a seasonal person that has come into and has now exited your inner circle. I need you to understand beloved that this pruning is absolutely mandatory. This is why it is so important to walk in the Spirit and not fulfill the lust of the flesh. I know that somebody is like "that sounds easy but". Love will truly be tested when you are going through this phase of the change. The people who have confessed their love for you in the past or present have to exercise the love that was confessed towards you. When somebody has love for you they only want the best for you at any cost. This could be them either deciding to change, or realizing that they would only be a distraction to your growth and extract themselves from your presence. The test is if we can make the cut off and not allow it to still become a distraction. I need you to understand that the flesh will not be accepting of this change but we are able to train our flesh into obedience. Hallelujah. This will take lots of work to accomplish and maintain, but it is well worth the wisdom and growth. I pray that any person that is associated with the wrong crowd is praying for deliverance from that bondage. The bonds that we form all throughout life have different levels of responsibility attached to them. This means that the kind of bonds we make in life have to be thoroughly evaluated decisions and not some hasty regret. We have to be careful of the ties we create. Soul ties can and surely will become our customized bondage if we are not careful. The tricky part is not to deceive ourselves. We have to be honest with ourselves and then later we can rejoice in the triumph that will be evidence of growth in the decision making area. This is all part of the process of deliverance. The only way to truly make it out is to make it through. Faith will carry us through any situation. We will be justified through grace and will overcome any bondage. I need to tell you though that flesh cannot be justified. Through the faith in his blood declare righteousness for the remission of sins and by grace we will be redeemed. We are the redeemed of the Lord and that is the anchor of promise. Hallelujah. Remember that all have sinned and come short of *The Glory Of God*. Okay I got it. The person without sin can throw their rock up towards the glass ceiling. Anybody want to go first?

S.K. Edwards

Knocking on heaven's door

His Grace & Mercy

God

S.K. Edwards

I looked up the meaning of God in the dictionary and it read, *"The creator and ruler of the universe and source of all moral authority"*, but he is so much more than that.

There is only one true and infinite God. The Alpha, and the Omega; ruler of all. Those that believe in him will have everlasting life.

Do you know what it means when God says "I'll be your God?" He means

When you are sick, I will heal you.

When you are broke, I will supply you.

When you are alone, I will stand by you

Simply when you need me I'll be your God.

There are people that question his existence. There are people that question his ability. I was always taught that everything is done for a reason, and not to question God's work.

He says, "Those who know me, know that if you need wisdom; all you have to do is ask.

His Grace & Mercy

I will give wisdom to everyone who asks in faith. Refuse to allow the issues of life to have preeminence. You must maintain eternal perspective and intimate relationship with me. Let nothing interrupt your flow in the Spirit."

That felt so good, let me say that again, "LET NOTHING INTERRUPT YOUR FLOW IN THE SPIRIT!!!

What you are not realizing is that flow has allowed you to make the right decision when the wrong one seemed better, keep going when giving up seemed like the best option.

I was asked one day what the difference in The Father, the Son, and the Holy Spirit? When I answered they are all the same person, she looked so confused that she shook her head and didn't want to hear any more.

Well if you don't know I guess I could see why that would confuse you, so let me explain.

God The Father: (The creator)
He created the heaven and earth and everything in it. Of all that was created, man was his greatest. He was so proud of man, that he gave man the ability to ascend upon the rest. Ascended enough to be one step below the angels. Once man disobeyed God, that began a downward spiral of evil that made God angry. Man was such a disappointment with his sin and wicked ways that God stopped talking to man. This lasted for 400 years.

God The Son: (The redeemer)

He loved man so much that he came in the form of his son, then put his plan of salvation into effect; which was Jesus dying on the cross for our sins.

John 3:16 says, "For God so loved the world that he gave his one and only son, that whoever believes in him shall not perish, but have everlasting life."

His Grace & Mercy

Jesus loves me this I know, for the bible tells me so.

God The Holy Spirit: (The Keeper)

There are a couple of scriptures that I have to reference with this one.

John 7:38, 39 says "Whoever believes in me, as the scripture had said, streams of living water will flow from within him." By this he meant the spirit, whom those who believed in him were later to receive. Up to that time the Spirit had not been given, since Jesus had not yet been glorified.

.This one goes back to when I said you have free will.

Were you ever about to do something wrong, and a little voice, or thought said that you shouldn't do that? Well, that's the Holy Spirit!

When you got saved, did you get to the point, to what people had to say about you didn't matter? That's the Holy Spirit!

S.K. Edwards

The Keeper reminds you how to live for God, and helps you get past public opinion when you do.

John 14:25-29 These things I have spoken to you while being present with you. [26] But the Helper, the Holy Spirit, whom the Father will send in My name, He will teach you all things, and bring to your remembrance all things that I said to you. [27] Peace I leave with you, My peace I give to you; not as the world gives do I give to you. Let not your heart be troubled, neither let it be afraid. [28] You have heard Me say to you, 'I am going away and coming back to you.' If you loved Me, you would rejoice because I said,[a] 'I am going to the Father,' for My Father is greater than I.

[29] "And now I have told you before it comes, that when it does come to pass, you may believe.

His Grace & Mercy

The Wrong Hands

S.K. Edwards

When I say I grew up in church, I mean the kind of church that Steve Harvey often talked about in comedy shows.

Tuesday and Thursday were bible study. Friday and Saturday was choir rehearsal. Then there was Sunday. We went to Sunday school from nine to eleven. Then service started at eleven thirty until two (Unless it was first Sunday). We left church and went to my grandmother's house to eat dinner, then it was back to church at six. Sometimes the evening service lasted until ten; even on Monday and Wednesday, we, sometimes, had bible time at home.

Back then I didn't understand why we were in church so much. See, we lived in the worst part of Richmond, at what was considered the worst time Richmond has seen. Now I understand that my mom was trying to protect us from the streets, by keeping us covered in the blood of Jesus.

At 15, I started working at a local Kmart, so I would buy nice clothes to wear to church. I was proud of what I was doing, that is until one of the deacons came to me about me selling drugs. I was not only offended by the accusation, but hurt by the oversight of what I considered an accomplishment for Christ. So I shied away from church and did my own thing.

That lasted for a couple of years until I met this girl, who just happen to be a preachers' daughter. As the daughter of a minister, she was required to attend church, and since the church wasn't far from my house, I went in order to see her. The more I went, the more I started to miss my upbringing, so I got more involved until I was back into the swing of things. The church was a little different. We didn't go as much, but the lessons were the same, and that's all that really mattered. She was cool with the fact that I was a single father, but some of the people in the church weren't as accepting. They would make negative comments about a man raising a little girl, teenage parents, how I was a bad influence, stuff like that. Again, I left wondering was this a sign that church wasn't for me.

Three years later, my grandfather died. At his funeral, the preacher that delivered his eulogy gave such an inspiring message that I decided to give his church a try. By now I'm 20, and engaged to my second daughters' mother. She was four months into her pregnancy when I was baptized and became hands on involved in the church. That is until one Sunday the preacher was giving the benediction prayer, and said, "Lord I want you to bless the unborn baby of this couple, even though it's a bastard, because they are not married.

I was floored. Needless to say, that was my last Sunday under his leadership. It took the next eighteen years, to realize that I put my faith in the wrong hands. Instead of letting someone's opinion run me away from the one person who love's me unconditionally, I should have used that negativity as fuel to grow stronger in his presence. I learned the hard way that my

His Grace & Mercy

worst day with God is a million times better than my best day without him.

S.K. Edwards

That heavenly Journey

His Grace & Mercy

THE BATTLE WITHIN

S.K. Edwards

Okay, here we go. Right away go to Mark 9: 19 – 27 and read. Sometimes we think that what's going on inside of us is bad but it could be good for us. Pay attention to the area where you are being attacked, because this is the area where you have it going on. We have to remember that sometimes the enemy is the "inner me". We have a tendency to be our personal biggest enemy. This is a very large flag indicating an extreme lack of faith. This is what happens when we get our minds filled with negative thoughts or listen to negative that's being spoken into our situations or over our lives. This is also an indicator of doubt. Go to Mark 11:21 – 24 right now but don't forget to come back to the book. I understand how addictive the bible can be. When you read those verses you realize how important it is not to doubt but to believe. Okay, if you really want to see how important this is flip your bibles back to Matthew 21: 21. The same word was spoken by God to the people. That shows consistency right there. Things that are

His Grace & Mercy

really important or what we call nuggets are stamped into our spirits like book marks. The problem is getting us in the spirit realm, and then staying there long enough to see anything manifest. Manifestation is the end result of your process, but this to hinges on where our belief is. This is why it is important to believe in our hearts and not let our minds have us in a state of confusion. We have to make some of the most crucial decisions in our hearts and we cannot let our thoughts get us off track. This is powerful reinforcement right here. We have to turn over to Matthew 14: 31, but go back and read this chapter because there you will learn how strong we have to be in the midst of whatever we might have going on in our lives. Peter was at a crucial moment in life where he had made a decision in his heart with faith but allowed his head and doubt to have input that ultimately had an effect in the outcome of his situation. I often wonder if Peter would have lost faith and doubted if he would have known everything that had happened up until that moment when Jesus came to them on the water. I believe that all of them would have jumped out of the boat and went to meet Jesus on the water had they known. They would have realized that the anointing for seeing and doing the impossible was available at that moment. Jesus had encountered and overcome tragedy with triumph, and it totally changed the course of the day. We have to keep doubt on the way out and faith coming in at all times. This could very well change the outcome of the day and ultimately your life.

While we are talking about faith right now let's reinforce doubt with faith now. We have to go back to Matthew if we closed our bibles. The bible should be in reach at all times while reading this book, because there will be scripture chasing going on at a high rate. Okay in Matthew 14: 32, something amazing happened that a lot of us probably missed before. This scripture reads as such "And when they were come into the ship, the wind ceased." This was like a combat training exercise ending. The wind stopped only after Peter lost faith and Jesus caught him. Peter had failed a faith exercise that could have been a monumental point in his life. Peter had missed the shift. That is why in verse 31 Jesus made a comment that had the tone of disappointment. Jesus said" O thou of little faith, wherefore didst thou doubt?" It makes you wonder if Jesus expected for Peter to have no doubt that he could have walked on the water. This is an example of how somebody might feel if they had no doubt that we would succeed, but our personal doubt made all the difference in the outcome of the situation. We can't just step out and into a situation, we have to step up to and then over the situation. Stepping up to the situation is taking it head on. Stepping over the situation automatically gives faith dominion over the situation and paralyzes fear or doubt in the situation. We are more than conquerors because we have a victory Spirit inside of us. We are over comers of what is before us. I say this because, we don't just have a piece or some measure of the Holy Ghost, we are filled with it. This should override any doubt at all. Okay I got it. Let's flip to Galatians 5:1. This is a nugget. "Stand fast therefore in the liberty wherewith Christ hath made us free, and be not entangled again with the yoke of bondage". Wow. Hallelujah. Hallelujah. We have liberty given to us by Christ. That is or should be the end of this discussion. Bondage had been made captive at that moment. Doubt is a form of bondage right? Right, so it has been made captive as well. We have allowed our lack of knowing how empowered we are to become a giant. Make the devil out of a liar in every situation. Praise God in the midst of your situation and confuse the enemy. Okay, now go to verse 13 of this same chapter of Galatians and you get more insight. When you get down to verse 17 stop. It reads:"For the flesh lusteth against the Spirit, and the Spirit against the flesh: and these are contrary the one to the other: so that ye cannot do the things that ye would". STOP. STOP. STOP. This means that as long as you allow your mind or the doubts of your mind to creep in and you become bondage to that thing that was in bondage. We have liberty and we have to use it or lose it. We should operate in confidence at all times. In most cases the Spirit can solve the problem if we would just step aside and give it room to operate. We must allow ourselves to be renewed by the transforming of our minds. We must renew our minds and our mindsets. We can and shouldn't expect something for nothing but most of us do. We think that everything is as it should be but we are deceiving nobody but ourselves. Change promotes change and faith promotes faith. We can however allow our faith to lead us to the changes that are necessary.

The battle in our minds is sometimes something to talk about and sometimes it requires us to talk to our Lord of Lords, God the Father through prayer. Don't allow what you are going through to stop you from where you are going to. We are tested and tried so much and in so many ways when we are going through our growth process. We have to focus on our lives on the other side of the situation. What we have to go through is just that, something we are going through. We have to find hope and give thanks to God that we have a promise in his word. This too shall pass or be passed as we advance. That's right family, we are going to press our way into the breakthrough that awaits us. The worship and praise that we push from our spirit can literally shift the atmosphere in the natural. We could witness the yokes of bondage to fall from our necks because of the anointing. We have to keep on pushing to the good and through the bad with our praise and worship. Stopping is not an option in us reaching our destiny. We have to keep our minds stayed on the love of God and his good measure that is pressed down from heaven upon our lives. We don't have time to stop and take time away from our praise and worship, to entertain another dramatic scene of flesh and ignorance on display. Okay check this out,

His Grace & Mercy

flip over to Romans 8: 24-28. I can't let you lose this nugget by any means necessary. Read. "For we are saved by hope: but hope that is seen is not hope: for what a man seeth, why doth he yet hope for? But if we hope for that we see not, then do we with patience wait for it. Likewise the Spirit also helpeth our infirmities: for we know not what we should pray for as we ought: but the Spirit itself maketh intercession for us with groaning which cannot be uttered. And he that searcheth the hearts knoweth what is the mind of the Spirit, because he maketh intercession for the saints according to the will of God. And we know that all things work together for good to them that love God, to them who are the called according to his purpose." Hallelujah. Hallelujah. God you are so worthy of all praise. I exalt you God. I lift you up Lord. Lord I love you and bless your name. God you are so awesome. Hallelujah. The worry and doubt is leaving you now. Hallelujah. The hurt and pain that you have been experiencing day after day is over. Hallelujah. We were not given the spirit of fear, but the power of love and a sound mind. Thank you Father God. I want you to refer to right here if you ever can't begin to praise and worship God. I stand in agreement with you right now for your situation to break right now. Hallelujah. Glory unto the highest God. What can separate us from the love of Christ? NOTHING at all. I know that sometimes we have anxieties and uneasy feelings, but what do our feelings have to do with our faith? NOTHING AT ALL. This uneasy feeling in your Spirit is probably just how it seems, or how your situation is, uneasy. We can either get stopped and make ourselves vulnerable for attacks simply by being out of the will of God for our lives or stay focused. We have to let these things pass us by with none of our time or energy invested. Sometimes these things should be discerned meaning that it has none of our concern. When you discern something this means that you have decided that this thing or situation does not require us to be attentive to it. I am hopeful that each of us

His Grace & Mercy

will learn at some point how to not concern ourselves to be distracted. Distractions are the result of not letting something pass. Why instead, would we allow distractions to take us away from where our attention should be? Check this out family. I just got this hot off the wire concerning the things we just discussed. I hope we all are still in Romans but if you are not still there do it now. This is a scripture chase to what I said earlier. Romans 8: 35-37. I know you thought I was going to give you the scripture and you are correct. "Who shall separate us from the love of Christ? Shall tribulations, or distress, or persecution, or famine, or nakedness, or peril, or sword? As it is written, for thy sake we are killed all the day long; we are accounted as sheep for the slaughter. Nay, in all these things we are more than conquerors through him that loved us." Hallelujah. This is praise above all praise. This is why that thing or situation was none of your concern at all. Emotionalism and excitement must not and cannot come before expectation. Okay on one end we have Proverbs 10: 28;" The hope of the righteous shall be gladness: but the expectation of the wicked shall perish." This is the beauty of being in the will of God. The same is true on the other end. Romans 10: 11-14 which says; "The mouth of a righteous man is a well of life: but violence covereth the mouth of the wicked. Hatred stirreth up strifes: but love covereth a multitude of sins. In the lips of him that hath understanding wisdom is found: but a rod is for the back of him that is void of understanding. Wise men lay up knowledge: but the mouth of the foolish is near destruction. The mouth of the foolish is already headed for an expected end that you don't have to worry about. What we do have to worry about is what it is we are really trusting God for. What actually is our expectancy? Does our faith meet or exceed whatever it is that we are expecting? Whatever we are thinking should be magnified. Wow let's stay here for one second, because I just found a nugget. Okay, if our thoughts should be magnified

His Grace & Mercy

and we should have God on our minds at all times, doesn't that mean we should automatically magnify God? Amen. Can I get a witness? Can I get anybody to come into agreement with me on this? Hallelujah anyway. Let's go to Ephesians 3: 20. This reads; "Now unto him that is able to do exceeding abundantly above all that we may ask or think, according to the power that worketh within us." Wow! That's why the next verse says that unto God be the glory in the church by Christ Jesus throughout all ages, world without end, and then says Amen. That's a nugget that we should highlight in our spirits. That which is promised shall be made manifest in our lives when it is in God's will. Stop and give God a hand of praise and thanks right now. God is worthy of our praise because he is so awesome in fulfilling his promises to us that believe. Wait a minute; I just got something in my spirit. We have to go back to that scripture Ephesians 3: 20. The last part of that scripture is big. The latter part might be bigger the key that we have missed many times in our expectancy. God can and is able to do exceeding abundantly more than we could ask or think only by the power that works within us. I hope you got that. The power that is being referred to here is our faith. This means that we can't blame God or anybody else for things not happening for us. We are made accountable because of the level of faith we are approaching our expectancy with. We often have to change our approach to situations. We have to flow with the move of God that's happening in that season. I hope that you who may be reading this book have already read Wise Words Spoken, the first part to this book. I have the information in the back of this book to assist you in adding that to your arsenal. Okay, in that book I talked about how we grow from faith to faith. I will do you one better. Let's turn over to Romans 1: 17. This says "For therein is the righteousness of God revealed from faith to faith: as it is written, the just shall live by faith." Hallelujah and Amen. Can you imagine the righteousness of God being

His Grace & Mercy

revealed to you on any level of faith that you can believe on? There is no possible way that we can beat God's giving potential, but we can posture our spirits to make us qualify for different levels of right and just favor being executed in our lives. Hallelujah. This is my personal reason for not being ashamed of the gospel "good news" of Christ the risen king. Do you even realize that you are holding your family back? We slack and that slack slides down the family tree. I declare over your life right now that you can be made free of anything that you are faithful enough to believe. I mean dig in and stand steadfast in your faith and you will surely reap the benefits of it. When we see God moving through our faith, we have to allow our faith to go up to another level believing that we are going to where our faith goes and better yet that God is meeting us there. I dare you to trust God and let your faith explore higher levels of faith. When our faith is aroused it will actually reward us with more faith. Things will begin to happen that are out of the norm when favor gets to where our faith is. The anointing on the situation is definitely the difference in results. God will only command a blessing where he told you to be. Don't let anybody or anything move you from where God told you to be. Stand still where God told you to stand. Stay in God's will for your life. Stop asking people for conformation about what God said. That which was ordered over your life by God will not return not done. Who can give us better assurance than God? Listen, if somebody tells you they can give more assurance than God, run. We have to be careful not to frustrate or fall from the grace of God. Watch your complaints and whining while in the will of God. What is the wisdom in playing around outside of the will of God? When we are inside of the will of God we are empowered to prosper. This empowerment can be referred to as favor being on our lives. We have access to the unstoppable blessings of heaven. Can you imagine being totally soaked with the favor of God? Congratulations, because you are worthy of this favor. I pray that all would stay in the will of God, but the good news is that because of the grace and mercy God will still ease his will from you slowly. God wants us to stay on the path that contains all he has for us. We were made for God by God. We were created for God's pleasure. We should be consumed with excitement at the opportunity to be used by God. When you are in the will of God, things flow easier for you. Everything flows on another level when you get in the will of God. When you are not in the will of God, it is evident because things get all hung up and difficult for you. The Holy Spirit has to be in the midst of what you are trying to do. God has to be the guidance and director of what you are doing telling us how and what to do. The steps must be ordered by God. People don't plan to fail, but they fail, or forget to include God in the plan. When God says it, it's done. The plans we have are no good if they are not in the will of God for you. We will miss our blessings outside of his will. I believe that if we will be obedient and willing we will prosper. Amen. We also have to be very careful of the people around us because if they are out of the will of God it could affect us. We have to be mindful of our soul ties and associations. We have to always remember that we are rewarded for our obedience. The reward for obedience on your life is known as favor. Wow. Somebody needs to know what I'm talking about. Amen. Hallelujah God. When you just praise God at all times you gain favor. This sounds like a word of wisdom. Let's go...

His Grace & Mercy

Prayer

S.K. Edwards

Being raised in church we prayed every day. So I was floored the first time someone told me that they didn't know how to pray. What I explained was prayer is just a conversation with God.

Father I pray right now that you would make us more aware of the power of prayer. God we thank you for keeping us when we can't keep ourselves. We pray for wisdom and insight into the things of you God. We ask God that you teach us how to react properly when we feel pressure or diverse attacks from the enemy. We pray God that you would continue to teach us how to be spiritual. We thank you for teaching us that trouble won't last always God. We pray that just a little talk with you God will make everything better. We thank you God for the Holy Ghost, which is our comforter that you sent us from Heaven just for us. We pray that you would unlock the power of prayer and give us knowledge that passes all understanding. We thank you in advance God for what you are about to do in our lives. We know God that prayer will change things and we give you permission God to make the necessary changes needed to get us where you want to be. We give you glory, honor, and praise now in Jesus' strong and mighty name, Amen.

Okay, so now let's get free and get a fresh understanding as it pertains to prayer. We have heard that prayer changes things but why does prayer change things? I pray that prayer is going to become made plain and we all get a piece of information that helps us become powerful prayer warriors. We have heard people pray and it seemed to have grabbed us and taken us to another level. I pray that someone who may not know how to pray learns to pray prayers with power and purpose. A prayer is a petition that we place before God. A prayer is one of the single most important weapons we need in our spiritual arsenal. Let's go to Matthew 6: 5-8 which reads, "And when thou prayest, thou shalt not be as the hypocrites are: for they love to pray standing in the synagogues and in the corners of the streets, that they may be seen of men. Verily I say unto you, they have their reward. But thou, when thou prayest, enter into thine closet, and when thou hast shut thy door, pray to thy Father which is in secret; and thy Father which seeth in secret shall reward thee openly. But when ye pray, use not vain repetitions, as the heathen do: for they think that they shall be heard for their much speaking. Be not ye therefore like unto them: for your Father knoweth what things ye have need of, before ye ask him." I think if we didn't get anything else about prayer we got a massive nugget just now but I must thoroughly teach you the things of God. The people perish for lack of knowledge. I really believe that prayer is the one area where we have to be given insight. I give all glory to God for what' about to go down. We are about to learn how to properly place our petition of prayer before God. This is one of the most important prayers you will recite in your life. I was raised standing in my

His Grace & Mercy

kitchen floor as a child reciting this prayer. My family would then and still on Sunday mornings lock hands and go to God with this corporate prayer, followed by a scripture and then the blessing of the food we were about to receive. This is none other than the Lord's Prayer. This is found at Matthew 6: 9-13 and reads, "After this manner therefore pray ye: Our Father which art in Heaven, Hallowed be thy name. Thy kingdom come. Thy will be done in Earth, as it is in Heaven. Give us this day our daily bread. And forgive us our debts, as we forgive our debtors. And lead us not into temptation, but deliver us from evil: For thine is the kingdom, and the power, and the glory, forever. Amen." The bible, in the next couple of verses goes a little more into detail and that is why most people substitute "debtors" with "trespasses". Take the time to study what the word says in those following verses. We have to go before God with the honor and respect due unto him. This is God that you are about to try to pray to. This is the same God that created the heavens and the Earth and everything thereof. The Bible even tells us how we could get the problems of this land fixed. This information is found in 2 Chronicles 7: 14, which reads, "If my people, which are called by my name, shall humble themselves, and pray, and seek my face, and turn from their wicked ways; then I will hear from heaven, and will forgive their sin, and will heal their land." Okay stop for a moment. We have to get this right here. We would like to thank you Father for your eternal wisdom. Hallelujah. This is the blue print of reverence we should have for God. The Lord's Prayer is probably the perfect example of giving God glory, thanks, honor, and praise all wrapped up in one powerful package. Listen to the words of power that are easily identified because they are masterfully sculpted words. A person could easily make the argument that people had more respect for the power of God. People took off their shoes when they stepped on holy ground. People pressed their way to the place where the next miracle was supposed to happen. They didn't have the luxury of depending on the city, state, or federal government to solve every problem. They had no plans but for God to make a way for them. They prayed with a lot of substance and meaning in their prayers. Let's go to James 5: 15 and 16 to get some revelation knowledge. These scriptures read, "And the prayer of faith shall save the sick, and the Lord shall raise him up; and if he have committed sins, they shall be forgiven him. Confess your faults one to another, and pray one for another, that ye may be healed. The effectual fervent prayer of a righteous man availeth much." Did you just read that? There is even a prayer of faith. This particular prayer would heal the sick and the sinner. This prayer also says that this person will be raised up. This is the actual meaning of deliverance. This is being healed from all sickness and being totally forgiven for all sins, and then being raised up. I believe that being raised up is a promotion of some sort. This sounds like we can go to another level through this prayer. Faith itself is an action word. Faith is for doers. Praying is for doers also. This should be the way that we are. We should not worry but instead pray. We should be believers of whatever it is that we pray for. We are growing in these areas at the same time and the proof is that your prayers have effect. A prayer of faith has enough power to endure whatever trials may be present in our lives. The glory will be the end result of your prayers. I believe that victory starts with a prayer and ends with a prayer of thanksgiving and praise. Wow, I just caught hold of something. A person with praise prays. Faith has to produce so it has to work. A prayer built and based on faith has to be the equivalent of a volcano. Imagine the believers that pray and praise while they are waiting for a prayer to come to manifestation. The praise is the energy that urges the volcano to erupt. We know that volcanoes need a lot of energy so faith has to stay high and steadied by a work of patience. Patience during your trial is accomplished by staying

His Grace & Mercy

focused and fixed on the other side of our prayers and actually moving within praise. When we are moving within praise we become invisible to every negative force that would or could prevent you from believing. We actually begin to gain endurance in our prayers. This gives us the ability to stand firm on our prayers with belief for results. Praise also confuses the enemy so this is an added bonus to having praise in our mouths instead of excuses and complaints. Check out this key kick starter for prayers. This doesn't say some or most prayers but all. This is found in *Luke 11: 2, which reads, "And he said unto them, when ye pray say, Our Father which art in Heaven, Hallowed be thy name. Thy kingdom come. Thy will be done, as in heaven, so in earth. Give us day by day our daily bread. And forgive us our sins; for we also forgive every one that is indebted to us. And lead us not into temptation; but deliver us from evil."* I dare any person reading this now to begin all your prayers with this scripture and stand firmly believing in what you pray. I know that the word of God is true so you can expect results when you pray in this manner. Blessed is every person hears the word of God and keeps it, so I expect that the believers will at least try this for themselves. Remember that the word says to study to show yourself approved. I can now hear this scripture differently from before. This sounds to me like it is saying that we should try God for ourselves and allow God to prove himself to every believer. We can pray to God for ourselves and allow him to work through our faith, belief, and expectancy. Try these prayers behind the above beginning found in Luke.

Prayer against Depression

Feel free to make it personal by saying me instead of us. I was just making it a corporate prayer.

Father protect us from ourselves when depression comes against us. Father we bind the spirit of depression and loose joy and peace in that place. We ask you Father for your presence in the midst of our hearts and minds. Keep the promises of your word in our hearts right now Lord. Allow us to meditate on your word both day and night God. We know that there are no hurts on Earth that Heaven cannot heal. We bless you God for who you are. We thank you for your endless love God. Hallelujah. May our Lord and savior Jesus Christ rest rule and abide over us now henceforth and forever more. This and all prayers we ask in Jesus' name. Amen

S.K. Edwards

Prayer for Peace

Father we ask you to receive this prayer for peace that we place before you. We bless you God for being Jehovah Shalom, the God of peace. Father we pray this prayer for the restoration of peace in and around our lives. Father lay your hands on our lives and give us peace that passes all understanding. God move us out of the way so that the necessary adjustments can be made in our lives to restore peace to us. Father give us a fresh anointing that will allow us to receive and rest in the peace that you have for us. I thank you in advance for what you are going to do and for all that you have done already. Father we know what you are able and capable of doing in our lives. We give you glory, honor, and praise for what you are about to do God. This and all prayers we ask in Jesus' name. Amen

How many of us have fallen from time to time? I have my hand up. We all have fallen short at some point or another. I believe that every saint has a past just as every sinner has a future. We all have that something inside of us that allows us to get back up again. This is the result of giving God all of us. When God has all of us we can be healed or delivered from anything. When we give a person or thing all of us we have a much smaller chance of getting back up. In fact, so many just decide that they are not able or capable of pulling themselves up by the boot straps and end their lives. This is the direct result of people falling victim to depression. Depression is a heavy load for some people to carry. The good news is that we all have something available to us that will lead depression away captive every time. I don't want you to just take my word for it so let's turn over to Psalm 32 and find all who are depressed a place to hide. The scripture Psalm 32: 7 reads, "Thou art my hiding place; thou shalt preserve me from trouble; thou shalt compass me about with songs of deliverance." Verse 11 reads, "Be ye glad in the Lord, and rejoice, ye righteous: and shout for joy, all ye that are upright in heart." Okay if you can't find anything good about life how about thanking God for life anyway. We have all heard that God will not put more on us than we can bare so what excludes you? Most of us have already had to deal with some of the moments in life that seemed too much but now we look back and thank God for bringing us through. These moments are going to shape us and make us stronger. Trials and tribulations come to knock us into a state of heaviness or depression but that all depends on how you decide to face this attack. The key is that when the righteous cry out for help the Lord hears them and delivers them from their troubles. The question is who do we say that we are? Do we call ourselves the righteousness of God or not? We have to keep our hearts and minds far f that desolate pit called depression. We have to keep praise and worship on our minds at all times. The moment we feel overwhelmed we should be quoting a scripture and reaching towards Heaven. God is able and well capable to bring us out of any state of

His Grace & Mercy

depression. We have to know that God is willing to reach down low to pick us up out of our pitiful state only if we are willing. We have to remember that the joy of the Lord is our strength. We are way too blessed to be stressed or depressed by any weapon that forms against us. We have to always remember that God is our refuge and our strong tower. God is our shield and our deliverance. We have to be of good cheer because then our spirit can operate at full capacity. We can quote the serenity prayer in our time of heaviness. The serenity prayer goes like this;" God grant me the serenity to accept the things I cannot change. Courage to change the things I can and Wisdom to know the difference." This is very simple but very strong at the same time. This simple prayer is capable of keeping us through whatever we might find ourselves facing. This is asking God to give us the ability to accept things that are out of our control. This prayer goes further by telling us to use courage to be bold enough to seek and secure change whenever we can. Then it concludes by telling us to make sure we seek, receive, and execute wisdom so we don't ever experience this again. I pray that we all will be strong in our time of weakness and when we are vulnerable to the attacks of depression. Amen. Hallelujah

His Grace & Mercy

"Prayer of Thanks"

Lord as we bow our heads & gather in your name just one more time,
We come with humble hearts.
We give thanks for all the beautiful blessings that you continue to bestow upon us.
We especially want to thank –you for each member of our family near and far.
May we carry them in our heart. LORD. only you alone know the personal struggles each of us have to endure,
but we ask that you continue to guide us through.
We promise that we will never question your plans for us.
Your WILL shall be done.
With faith; we'll take your hand & walk beside you.
We understand that your unconditional love will always keep us safe in your arms.
On this Day,
Please allow peace to enter our mind & joy within our heart.
Your grace & mercy endures forever Amen!

S.K. Edwards

A New Years Blessing

"DEAR LORD"
I come 2 thee giving thanks for another year. As I look back on the moments of yesterday, I must admit, some days I walk through the storm, but I always appreciate the sunshine. I know that I couldn't have made with you! DEAR LORD, I'm grateful that you continue to grant me angel wings. I know that I can fly anywhere & do anything. I understand that you love me for who I am. I ask that you allow the blessing to flow in my life. No matter where I attempt to go, may I always find comfort in your presence. May each step lead me closer to my dreams & even closer to you. This life is not my own, but I'm thankful that you have chosen me. I appreciate & share all the wonderful gifts you have unselfishly given unto me. The gift of love, family, & loyal friends who care. I ask that you keep me and those who are dear to me near your heavenly throne. I bow my head in humble thanks, and simply say. AMEN HAPPY NEW YEAR 2 ALL!

His Grace & Mercy

"GOD"

I come thee knowing that I am WEAK. I ask GOD that you renew my strength. Help me to walk in faith by holding your strong hand. I know that I can do anything. I understand GOD that my rich blessing are delivered in abundance and come from YOU alone.
I PROMISE to live FOR YOU. YOUR love for me is UNCONDITIONAL & I desire to breathe like fresh air. I thank YOU for everything I possess now and...
in the future. Please GOD, allow your angels to watch over me daily! Guide my feet closer to YOU GOD, may YOU open my heart to receive you. I know father that YOU see for who I am & who I desire to be. Allow me, to work through you. In time, my prayers shall be answered!
AMEN

S.K. Edwards

"GOOD MORNING"

My DEAR heavenly father blessed me to see this day, so I quietly knelt down upon my knees to pray.
I want to thank -you for the sweet flowers that grow in the grass, along with ITS wet dew, when I'm searching for the answers LORD, I know I can always call on YOU.
I'm far from perfection Yet, you love me anyway.
 in YOUR presence I vow to stay!
As I rise up pull the covers from over my hed, I take time to graciously bow my head.
 I'm asking that you lead me in the direction YOU desire for me to go, I already know that you have blessed me like no other
 please watch over, my DEAR friends and place your healing hands upon my mother,

JESUS I desire to wear you upon my sleeve

this way we'll always connected

& your love for me shall never leave.

Good morning!

AMEN!!!

His Grace & Mercy

"GOD GOT IT"

GOD GOT IT, I gave him all my burdens today, he told I'll only find the answers if I take time to quietly pray.

Dear LORD, life's problems are sometimes difficult to understand, I can't carry the load, I placed everything in your capable hands.

I don't worry or have any pain upon heart, I already know GOD got before I can pick it apart,

God, I am your child there's nothing you can do, I surrender my most precious things to you. Every night I go to bed, the first thought inside head is rest comfortably GOD got it !

AMEN...

S.K. Edwards

Stepping out on faith

His Grace & Mercy

The Big Con

S.K. Edwards

The greatest trick the devil has played was convincing people that he didn't exist; all the while poisoning the mind of those that knew no better. He comes to you in ways that will appeal to your desires.

Proverbs 8:32

"Now then my children, listen to me; blessed are those who keep my ways.

My foundation originated from church and learning the bible. So when my loved one, that had very little knowledge if any, started asking me questions about the bible and God's existence, I was shocked, then pleased, then excited.

We began to discuss the bible and addressing many questions for about three months, when she came to me excited one day, saying that she wanted to try this church someone told her about.

After her first visit she was excited to report that she and her children joined this church. My first thought was, "what church let's you join after one visit; bible study at that?"

His Grace & Mercy

I was a little apprehensive, but didn't want to discourage her, so I offered to go to Sunday's service to support this decision.

We got to church about thirty minutes after service started, and she called us out in front of everyone. Even though I knew it was inappropriate, I brushed it off.

Now a lot of churches get a little extra at offering time, so it wasn't too far out of the realm when they asked for donations to support several different funds. That is until she looked in the collection basket and didn't see a lot of money. This so called woman of God stopped the service and started yelling at the congregation. It was unreal. That was enough for me. I knew this was not a situation that was of God, but my loved ones insisted on giving it a chance. I started to pray that God would show them the right way.

A little over a month after they started to attending, Pam, one of the daughters, applied for a job in the school. The Pastor, who was also the principal had her volunteer for a trial period. Her reason was to make sure the job was for the love of children, and not just a paycheck.

This so called woman of God worked Pam 11 hours a day, 5 days a week. She would give her what she called, a love token of 50 dollars, then it increased to 75 dollars, eventually increasing it to 100 dollars. All the while giving her scriptures in her own words to clarify what she was doing.

When I showed Pam in the bible,

James 5:4 Indeed the wages of the laborers who mowed your fields, which you kept back by fraud, cry out; and the cries of the reapers have reached the ears of the Lord of Sabbath.

She asked the pastor about what I showed her, and the pastor told her not to listen to me, I was the devil trying to discourage her from being saved.

His Grace & Mercy

I immediately began to pray that God would give her a sign to show her that this was not where she was supposed to be. At the same time not let this experience discourage them from wanting to be saved.

The following Tuesday was the faculty school meeting. Pam came home laughing, saying, "I'm not going back to that church anymore."

When I asked her what happened to change her mind, she had to take a minute to catch her breath from laughing before she proceeded to tell us.

She said, "The meeting started late because parents were late to pick up their children. I got up to go to the bathroom, when I returned, the majority of the staff were in tears. The pastor notioned for me to sit down, as she continued her rant on this one person. She told this lady that she stands too close to her husband when she talks to him. She then told her, "I'm a pastor but a lady first." Then invited her outside if she had a problem with it.

Pam, then apologized to me for not listening. I asked her how she felt about being saved and the bible after this experience. She said, one thing that Pastor did teach me, is that the devil will come to you in any form that he think will capture your soul. The funny thing is the devil told on himself.

I thanked God for answering my prayers, and bringing them out of the clutches of Satan.

His Grace & Mercy

DENIAL

S.K. Edwards

Matthew 10:33

But whosoever shall deny me before men, him will I also deny before my Father which is in Heaven.

This is a planned and plotted trick and trap of the enemy. The giant spirit that gets people stuck in this foolish "God doesn't want me" mess is way out of hand. I also hear people say that they are "in too deep". This giant is really strong as a hand puppet on a wall when the light is cut off. Hallelujah is the highest praise both then and now. We can't afford to lose focus of what we know are proven facts in our lives. Denial is as simple as knowing something and portraying that you have no knowledge of what is, or has happened. Denial has a posture that is void of confidence. Denial will distort your perception of that particular event initially, but will rapidly become the dominant personality displayed. Check this out. A person can deny God by not only by what is said but by simply losing hope and replacing faith with

His Grace & Mercy

failure. Denial will become the mask from which you view life. This denial will bring with it a heavy dose of deception and cover ups. Let me break it down real quick. We know or should know that now faith is the substance right? Right. When you lose sight of your substance you are not operating in faith. I can say this because you get so caught up trying to find the substance and lose hope for it once you grow in anxiety and frustration. Denial is knowing that favor produces victory but not flowing in the favor or victory that is available to us all. Denial is also a sign of lack in the area of integrity. We have to be good stewards of our time, so why waste time in denial of anything or situation. Wow! I just had a revelation. This word is to be broken down and stood upon and not under it. Deny is to be viewed as de nigh. We should draw nigh to God and he will draw nigh to us. We might get caught up in the under tow of denial and completely fall out of the will of God for our lives. We become lost and take on the spirit of isolation and begin to forsake assembling with those you are usually around. Integrity was affected when we had the perfect opportunity to make the right decision whether we would have been seen or not. Denial will make you shy away into some dark corner of thought and self pity. When you allow denial to turn into deception you deny the connection you have with the Kingdom and the righteousness you were seeking as well. We have the power to turn denial into deliverance if we would only believe. Things happen in the spirit before they happen in the physical so maybe some of us need more discernment as part of our spiritual make up. Whatever we focus on will expand so when you focus on denial, whether of God or anything or situation. When you expand in denial you also expand in lies and might lose sensitivity of the truth and your

spirit. Favor is birthed through obedience so disobedience is not an option or excuse. Denial will leave you stranded away from truth and separated in transition with no provision. Accept truth and trust that a

His Grace & Mercy

transition will happen in the Spirit without the natural knowing what happened.

Let your glory fill the place we are in God. God rain down on us favor. Shower your spirit upon us Lord God. We thank you father for even considering us worthy of your favor. We ask for whatever we might need in our lives God that would give us access to every blessing intended for our lives. We bless you God. God give us your favor with the wisdom to maintain it. Keep us with a fresh anointing that will bless our lives with your presence God. This petition we place before you God in Jesus' name. Amen

Favor is the perfect posture from which we should ask with supernatural expectancy.

S.K. Edwards

There's always light in the darkest place

His Grace & Mercy

F.A.V.O.R

Faith. **A**llows. **V**ery. **O**ppulent. **R**eceiving

S.K. Edwards

Hallelujah right now. Stop and recognize the power of the true and living God. Let the redeemed of the Lord say "So". That's what you tell your haters when they plot against you. That's what you tell the people in your life that wrote you off and didn't know that God saw you qualified for favor. Hallelujah.

Okay let's get into this wise word. We know that now faith is the substance of things hoped for right? Wait. Please forgive me for not slowing down my spirit to tell you where this scripture was. Let's turn over to Hebrews 11: 1, and see what was said. It says, "Now faith is the substance of things hoped for, the evidence of things not seen." Notice that it says "now faith", not the faith you had then. This is not the faith that you turn on and off like a light switch. Can I get a witness? The faith that you have right now is the faith you need to get this favor. We have to understand something though. Look over in Hebrews again at Hebrews 11: 6, which says "But without faith it is impossible to please him: for he that cometh to God must believe that he is, and

His Grace & Mercy

that he is a rewarder of them that diligently seek him." How much you trust God has a lot to do with your faith. We have to stay mindful of where our faith is. We are the determining factor of what is made available to us by the level of faith we have. We have to believe in our hearts through our faith that God can do the super natural on our behalf. I will give you another nugget right now. When we believe a promise through faith, God will deliver your promise not only because it was promised, but because you took a leap of faith. When you believed that what was promised would come to pass you put your unshakable faith on that thing correct? Yes you did. That faith was a request to God to make it happen and the promise turned into the motivation for you to believe. The faith is what got the result. The faith we have is the key to what we receive and how big what we receive is. Sometimes we have to reposition our faith accordingly. This is why the just live by faith. The just believe truly that faith is a principle thing. Faith becomes second nature to us as we grow and mature as believers. Faith is the main ingredient to favor. I will tell you why. Without faith as the root of our favor, we can have the things right in front of us and not even believe it's there. I say that because, the word says that we should walk by faith and not by sight. This means that we have to have enough faith to expect things to be there in order to receive them, even if we don't yet see them. Faith allows us to believe and receive that very thing God wanted us to have. We get too deep sometimes and mess up the blessing with our wavering faith. This is why God is always doing something in our lives that requires faith. We have this earthly flesh that from time to time tries to block our blessings because of our senses. Can I get a witness right here? We wavered because of what we saw in somebody else's situation or what we heard about somewhere else. That has nothing to do with what God has for you at all. We have to pay attention to what is happening in our life. We might

His Grace & Mercy

have favor on our life and they might not. Hallelujah. We can always expect exceptions as the King's kids. We are set apart as the chosen and faithful. What happens in our lives happens because God knows we will give him the glory and praise. The testimonies will motivate faith and then when faith is aroused it will produce more faith. Hallelujah. We should praise God for who he is and not for what we want. Don't get it twisted all up saints. The same way we can receive favor through faith we can lose favor because we failed a faith assignment. Trust God at all times. Favor allows us to experience opulence in our lives. What is opulence? This is "the good life". This is when you thought you had a regular seat on the airplane, but then the flight attendant told you there was an empty seat for you in first class. Hallelujah. This is how you get called to the front of the line when you were near or at the back of the line. This is receiving on a level that far exceeds all that we might ask or think. Opulence on your life is the result of you submitting yourself to God and his perfect plan for your life. Favor is the hand of God on your life being made visible for all to see. Favor allows us to be fruitful in every area of our lives. Favor will multiply your faith. What do I mean by that you ask? What I mean is that favor will multiply our faith times whatever we believe. The outcome is that we subdue or walk in dominion in everything we are involved in. That is favor being executed on our behalf. When we submit ourselves to God he will supply all our needs and wants accordingly. Favor will allow us to be an ambassador for God. We should never allow our faith to be judged or limited according to the wisdom of men, but instead by the power of God. Hallelujah somebody. Okay, no man can limit your faith because the demonstration of the power of God on your behalf will be unexplainable and cannot be judged by man's wisdom. The only response will be respect for the revelation or favor you received that was made manifest by God. We have to be steadfast and faithful

His Grace & Mercy

because a force of favor only flows as a result of obedience. Be strong in your faith and allow possibility to be the proven process to your success. I say this because the word says that all things are possible to them that believe. That belief is faith and that faith is powered by favor and that favor is powered by God. Hallelujah. The promise is possible so press on towards your prosperity. Amen. Okay listen, if now faith is the substance then what was promised has solidarity. Remember that faith comes by hearing the word of God. We have to use our favor (dominion) and God will do the rest. God will back you according to his promises. Walk in the favor that God has for you. You have earned it. Hallelujah. Hebrews 10: 35 reads "Cast not away therefore your confidence, which hath great recompense of reward." Thank you Lord God. That confidence is our faith. Why would we want to lose favor because we grow weak in the area of faith? Favor definitely allows opulent receiving. We have to recognize our season of favor. The season of favor might not last forever so don't miss the move of God when it is happening. We have to allow God to adjust our faith to accommodate our favor. When you are in your season of favor it will be awesome. God will bring us to where we need to be in order to bless us but it all depends on our faith. Where is your faith? Is your faith expecting favor?

Favor will position us for take off but our faith will allow us to soar. Amen. Why don't you just spread your spiritual wings and take flight. Why don't you just soar?

S.O.A.R.

Seek. Obtain. Arise. Rejoice

Hallelujah. I bless you God. You are the true and living God. The word reads something like this in Psalm 63:1; "O God, thou art my God; early will I seek thee: my soul thirsteth for thee, my flesh longeth for thee in a dry and thirsty land, where no water is." Hallelujah. The blessed part comes in the next couple of verses. This is so awesome because we are told what we must seek. Ready? Here we go. The second verse reads, "To see thy power and thy glory, so as I have seen thee in the sanctuary". Can you feel what you are reading? How many of us have felt this way in life? How many of us have just wanted to witness the power and glory of God in our lives? I have. Hallelujah. This is just part of the forming of our spiritual wings but we still have to get to this next scripture to get the revelation. Okay saints let's go deeper. The third verse reads, "Because thy loving kindness is better than life, my lips shall praise thee". This is where you get your praise on and give thanks for revelation knowledge. Amen. If it is better than life and we have a chance to experience his loving kindness during life, we know now we have to praise God. Hallelujah. This is the highest praise folks. I bless the name of God every chance I get. We should wake up thirsty and looking for God to show up. I got another one for you though if you still don't yet see the revelation. We have to turn over to Matthew 6: 33, but before you do let's get one more scripture in right here because it's important. The fourth verse reads, "Thus will I bless thee while I live: I will lift up my hands in thy name." What are you waiting for? Didn't you just receive some instruction? Yes we did. This is a good chance to practice a basic instruction for soaring. Lift your hands. Good, okay now give God some praise right now. I don't care where you are right now reading this book I want your hands up praising God even if it's for a moment. Okay now let's get over to Matthew 6: 33 which reads" But seek ye first the kingdom of God, and his righteousness; and all these things shall be added unto you." This is a promise that we are entitled to only if we are obedient. If you are having a problem with this maybe you don't have the reverence for God that you should have. Can I get a witness or am I talking to you? We are going to be in pursuit for righteousness because that's where our freedom is. I got another scripture for you that will bless you if you let it sink in. Let's go to a book that a lot of people probably never heard of before. Let's turn to Lamentations 3: 25 that reads;"The Lord is good unto them that wait for him, to the soul that seeketh him." Hallelujah somebody. This scripture promotes patience and the reward to all that do wait on the Lord. The second thing that we have to do is to obtain something useful that will help us to soar. We have to make sure that we have everything necessary to soar. Let's flip over to another book in the Bible that a lot of people haven't heard of. I thank God for the assignment that has been bestowed upon me. I pray that none of you are left out of the move of God in our lives. Let's go over

His Grace & Mercy

to 1Thessalonians 5: 9, which says;"For God hath not appointed us to wrath, but to obtain salvation by our Lord Jesus Christ." Did you catch hold of that nugget? God wants us to have salvation and he proved it by allowing Christ to be crucified at Calvary for our sins so that we can obtain salvation. Hallelujah. We thank you God. I can't imagine where any of us would be if Christ hadn't died for our sins so that we might be able to obtain salvation. Do we appreciate salvation or do we take it for granted? While you are trying to come with an answer let's go to Hebrews 4: 16 and see what God has for us. This scripture reads as follows "Let us therefore come boldly unto the throne of grace, that we may obtain mercy, and find grace to help in time of need." We have to go boldly which means that we must go sure and steadfast to the throne of grace with confidence. Then we have to obtain mercy and find grace. This will all come to pass as we prepare ourselves to grow spiritual wings so that we can surely soar. The exchange for obtaining mercy and finding grace is that we have to be obedient towards helping in the time of need. Okay, so this means that unless we are delivered from selfishness we will not be able to soar because we do not satisfy the minimum requirements. This would be a sad situation indeed. We have to be willing to surrender to the will of God for our lives. The next thing we must accomplish in order to soar after we have sought and obtained is to arise. This means that we are almost ready to soar but we still have a little further to go in order to take flight. We have to get up and become a doer of the word and not just say what we will do. Faith without works is dead and soaring without arising is also. Let's go to the scripture and see what the word says to our spirits. We have to go to Psalm 68:1 which reads," Let God arise, let his enemies be scattered: let them also that hate him flee before him". This seems like something that is mandatory. We have to let God be lifted up. We lift God up by our praise and worship. God could just arise but because

His Grace & Mercy

of free will we must allow God to rise up in our lives so that he can operate on our behalf. When we let God arise all evil will surely scatter because God is the light and darkness can not dwell where light is. Amen. The promise here is that all our haters will flee as well. This is awesome because not only will God arise, but a new standard as well. Hallelujah. This sounds like wings that are about to get free enough to take flight but we still have one thing left to do. We have to rejoice. When we give God thanks and praise we gain the altitude possible to be able to soar. Let's go to Psalm 33: 21 and read "For our heart shall rejoice in him, because we have trusted in his holy name". This is powerful because here we learn that because we have trusted him we will rejoice in our hearts. We trust in God's holy name which is hallowed and sacred. We rejoice from our hearts because this is where our Spirit is. The trust that we have in God's holy name is the equivalent to our faith. Faith is the substance that is the wind beneath our wings. We can reach the higher heights by praising God. God will surely show his power through us if we allow ourselves to be used by God. We can rejoice every time we think about how good God has been to us. God is able and capable of easily getting us to the altitude needed to be able to soar. When we go over to Proverbs 23: 24, we find out how good it is to rejoice. The bible reads, "The father of the righteousness shall greatly rejoice: and he that begetteth a wise child shall have joy in him". Why would we not want to stand on this promise? We find out here that rejoicing is not only praise but it brings joy to our parents. This is reason enough for anybody to soar. Rejoicing is a contagious praise. The word tells us also to rejoice with them that rejoice, and to weep with them that weep. This makes us further understand just how connected we all really are. We truly are all a part of God's family. Soaring is not for the faint at heart because it is a faith exercise. We should associate with people who are soaring instead of those flopping around on the ground with

His Grace & Mercy

no take off. We have to be careful to not lose altitude because of our actions. We also are told in other places in the Bible to rejoice evermore. I don't know about you but as for me I want to soar as long and as far as I can. Soaring allows us to enjoy life without constantly working, but instead enjoying the sights and reaping all the benefits and advantages of being on another level in every area of our lives. I do believe that seeking, obtaining, arising, and rejoice is something worth working towards. Don't you want to be caught up in the air? Hallelujah

S.K. Edwards

Leave your troubles in his hands

His Grace & Mercy

One more Move

S.K. Edwards

There was a man named James that was on the edge of a breakdown. He had just lost his job, his wife, and found out he had Cancer, all in one day. "God what are you doing to me!?" He shouted into the night. "Is this my life? I can't take anymore. Please give me a sign if I'm meant for more than this." He waited and nothing happened. James went home, distraught about all of the day's events, and went straight to bed.

The next morning, James had decided, after not receiving a sign, that he was going to kill himself by jumping off of the roof of the Convention center; one of the highest points in his city. Upon entering the Convention Center, James noticed a sign that said, Art Exhibition tour, Free Admission. He didn't understand why, but James decided to take the tour before he met with his demise.

The tour guide went from room to room, explaining different portraits by various artists until they came across picture that everyone thought was odd.

It was a picture of God and the devil playing chess. What made the painting so odd was that the devil had God at check.

His Grace & Mercy

Everyone mumbled for minute, about how weird it was for the devil to beat God at chess, then they moved on; well everyone except James. He couldn't take his eyes off of the picture.

 After a minute it hit him. He shouted out, "hold up everybody, come back. The game is not over, there's one more moved." Everybody turned and came back to see what James was talking about. It turned out that there was one more move to make, and God won.

So keep in mind, no matter how bad things may seem, as long as you keep the faith and believe, there's always one more move.

S.K. Edwards

I want to turn now to a subject that will surely set you up for a blessing. The thing that I am talking about can be actually offered up to God as a sacrifice. This is part of the dynamic duo that gets us ready for the word every Wednesday and Sunday or even Saturday if you worship on that day. This is always present with praise. The thing that I am talking about is Praise. Hallelujah.

His Grace & Mercy

P.R.A.I.S.E.

Proudly rejoice and indulge self evolution

S.K. Edwards

Okay let's get right into it. We should give ourselves away to praising and worshipping God. Praise God every time that you think about how good God is and has been to you and your family. I have seen people flat with their praise and I would attribute that to people actually losing their sensitivity to the presence of God. God loves to receive all our praise. We were created to praise God. God is going to get his praise from us one way or another so it's easier for us to just offer up our praise as a sacrifice unto God. We owe God all of our praise, glory, and all honor. It all actually belongs to God anyway. We have to be careful not to ever fail in giving God his praise. Never let people stop you from praising God. I actually would call it disrespectful to not praise God. We have to and should enter into his presence with praise and thanksgiving. Sometimes God might even hold back something from us for not giving him the praise he is due. Don't you think that God deserves all of our praise and worship, after all is said and done it belongs

His Grace & Mercy

to him anyway? Hallelujah. Praising God also includes giving him our time. We have to give God time so we have a chance to hear what he might want to say to us or through us. We should give God at least fifteen minutes of our day as a sign of respect and honor. Sometimes we have to train our flesh to honor God. When we praise God he will show us his power. We have to praise God because he is able and well capable to see us through any situation. The Lord, he is our God and he is worthy to be praised. We should praise God even if he never does another thing for us because he has already done enough. God has all power and all glory. All of our praise belongs to God. We have to provoke the presence of God through our praise. When we praise God his glory will show up. God's glory is full of his goodness. We have to praise God no matter what our current position might be. We all are able to praise God through our faith. We must poise ourselves for praise and live on purpose because of the promises of God. Praise is powerful enough to confuse the enemy. We have to praise God for not only what he has done in our past and our present but also our future. We have to praise God in advance for whatever we are expecting him to do on our behalf. We have to stay poised, prepared, and positioned to praise God. Praise can also change the perception of what we see and how we see things. We have to make sure that we praise God with our whole heart. We learn from Psalm 34: 1, that we must bless the Lord at all times and his praise should continually be in our mouth. The Bible also teaches us that we can praise God through singing and dancing our praise to him. When we look at the forty second chapter of Psalm we learn that even the countenance of God is due our praise. Hallelujah is the highest praise. This in it's broken down form means "Praise be unto God", and this is a very powerful weapon to have in your spiritual arsenal. This is definitely a word of wisdom. This is what you can say when you just don't know what to say. This is a word of the faithful and the worship for the believers. Okay here we go, let's get over to Psalm 63: 3, thank you Holy Spirit. This reads, "Because thy loving kindness is better than life, my lips shall praise thee". Hallelujah. This is talking about not just God's love but also his kindness towards us. This is described as being better than life. This to me means that it is better to be in the love and kindness of God, than to have life at all. Wow. What faith it takes to stand on that kind of promise. This is why his praise will be on our lips at all times. Okay, but drop down through the next two scriptures and find a blessing for your Spirit. "Thus will I bless thee while I live: I will lift up my hands in thy name". This means that because God has allowed us to live we should lift our hands and praise God with a shout of praise. The next scripture is a powerful one. This one reads, "My soul shall be satisfied as with marrow and fatness; and my mouth shall praise thee with joyous lips". Did you notice how the scripture shifted into praise? Here not only is praise on just regular lips, but the praise is now on joyous lips. How many of us need to upgrade our lips to joyous lips? My hand is lifted up right now. Where is my witness? Can I get a witness? Praise is who I am. Who are you? I believe it is better to praise than to complain. We could be praising with the same breath that we are wasting with complaints. The praise that we place before God can shift the atmosphere. Breakthroughs and deliverance for any of our situations can all depend on the praise and worship we offer to God. The power of praise and worship together can move, break, and tear down whatever strong holds might be blocking you. We also learn in God's word that we should make our praise glorious before God. Flip over to Psalm 67, around the third and fifth verses and we see praise in the form of a petition placed before God. This scripture reads, "Let the people praise thee, O God; let all the people praise thee". This is like a prayer for God to accept our praise. Praise is even referred to as a garment for the spirit of

His Grace & Mercy

heaviness over in Isaiah in 61. I find the book of Psalms to be one book in the Bible where we could get a doctorate in praise. Take a look over in Psalm 145, and read a paramount scripture concerning praise. This scripture reads, "Great is the Lord, and greatly to be praised; and his greatness is unsearchable". Hallelujah high praise be unto God. Praise God in privacy if you want to experience a moment of total praise. We find out in life that sometimes we have to praise God by ourselves. This is helps to build solidarity in our personal relationship with God. Who would want to miss out on this party? A praise party is the best party you could ever want to be present at. Just imagine the line wrapped around the corner for believers who are trying to get in a praise party. Let's get to the next chapter and uncover another power pellet of praise. The first and second verse reads as such, "Praise ye the Lord. Praise the Lord, O my soul. While I live will I praise the Lord: I will sing praise unto my God while I have any being." Wow, when we jump to the next chapter we catch another power pellet. This verse reads, "Praise ye the Lord: for it is good to sing praises unto our God; for it is pleasant; and praise is comely." I cannot believe what I have just realized. The beginning of every chapter starting at chapter 146 straight through to 150, all begin with the word "praise" in the first verse. I could give you each one but I want you to earn your degree in praise. I challenge you reading this book to take it upon yourself and see if what I am saying is true. The word says that we should study to show ourselves approved. I don't want you to ever just depend on what somebody says, I want you to check it out for validity. Whoa! I just ran across a nugget in the form of a reward for praise. We have to turn over to chapter 149 of the book of Psalm. There the fourth verse reads, "For the Lord taketh pleasure in his people: he will beautify the meek with salvation." Hallelujah. You had better praise God for his mighty acts and his excellent greatness. I don't care how you choose to praise God I know you better catch hold to the principle of praise. Salvation is just one of the rewards that are set aside for praise and worship warriors. We are more than conquerors because of God and for that reason he deserves our praise. We can praise God in our own special way. Praise God through your life or through your gifts as long as you praise God in some way, shape, or form. When we say that we honor God did you know that was another way of giving God praise? Praise can be simple and very far from a complicated task to perform. We can find another massive spiritual nugget over in the book of Proverbs concerning praise that will save us from making a huge mistake. Let's make our way to 27: 2, and grab hold of this wisdom. This verse reads, "Let man praise thee, and not thine own mouth; a stranger, and not thine own lips." Don't stop praising him now. This means that we shouldn't go around praising ourselves. We have to train our flesh into obedience. When we turn over to Philippians, we find out that even in the way we think praise should be present.

S.K. Edwards

The scripture found at Philippians 4: 8 reads, "Finally, brethren, whatsoever things are true, whatsoever things are honest, whatsoever things are just, whatsoever things are pure, whatsoever things are lovely, whatsoever things are of good report; if there be any virtue, and if there be any praise, think on these things." This in a nut shell gives us a complete rundown on the kind of thoughts we should have going on in our heads. When we can get to this way of thinking, I know that a majority of us would see a big difference in our lives just based on what we are thinking about. I pray that this information is not only helpful but used as a foundation for change. I want you to also remember that your victory is in your praise. Things begin to be changed and rearranged when we keep praise present. I know that things get rough sometimes and it seems hard, but all you have to do is begin to praise God. Proper praise promotes power, promise, and provision. Try saying that really fast. Hallelujah.

His Grace & Mercy

I am so filled with praise right now. I realize that sometimes we might get so caught up in our daily grind that when attacks come we panic instead of praise. I also know that for one reason or another; a lot of people feel powerless when certain things come up against them. We have to hold on to our spiritual principles when the pressures of life are penetrating our peace. We have to know what to do when we lose spiritual consciousness and are in need of spiritual first aid. We are left vulnerable to diverse attacks from the arsenal of the enemy when we don't know what to do. I know of one thing that is able and well capable of getting you back to stability and restoring us when we are in need of spiritual first aid. This one thing is prayer. I really hope that your needs are being met and that you are better, stronger, and wiser. Let's get into prayer and free ourselves as we arm our spirits with kingdom weaponry. The word teaches us that the weapons of our warfare are not carnal. This means that we use a different type of weapons to fight the good fight.

S.K. Edwards

Know that you are not traveling that road alone

A.S.S.I.S.T.

All. **S**ufficient. **S**avior. **I**s. **S**till. **T**here

S.K. Edwards

HALLELUJAH... Let's get straight into a flow with the Holy Spirit right now. We all have a reason to praise God already. What else explains the almighty father but ALL? We know that God is our all and all. Amen? I only want us to say "Amen" because we agree with what was said. We should have a clear understanding of what we are coming into agreement with before we declare that it is so. When you say that you are in agreement with what was said and that it possibly was spoken over your life, God forbid you allow it over your family. This is why we should be wise enough to trust in our all sufficient savior. God is the Alpha and the Omega. God is the beginning and the end. God is the Author and Finisher of our lives. God is all knowing, seeing, and present. God is our provider, healer and prince of peace. God is the reason that we made it through. Can you declare out of your mouth that no matter what it cost you and no matter how many scars you have gotten on your way through your process that it must be worth it? Can we stand as

His Grace & Mercy

the body of Christ and declare to the world that we know it will work out to our good because we believe? Can I get somebody to stand and be counted as a witness of the power that God has. God can deliver and mend our lives if we only trust and believe that he can. God can and will do more if we expect more. We are about to get somebody free right now. When all else fails the all sufficient savior is still there. When we try it over and over and come to the same dead end our all sufficient savior is still there. When the doctors walked out and said that nothing else could be done our all sufficient savior is still there. When we get down to the last possible second and the future is totally out of our hands our all sufficient savior is still there. When we find ourselves in the middle of every one of life's tests, trials, or tribulations our all sufficient savior is still there.

S.K. Edwards

The calming of the stormy waters

His Grace & Mercy

B.A.D.

Blessed **a**nd **D**elivered.

S.K. Edwards

1. When the enemy tries to attack you, just remember that you are B.A.D. 2. When things don't seem to be going right on your job, just remember that you are B.A.D. 3. When things are not looking good in your marriage or relationships, just remember that you are B.A.D. 4. When people scandalize your name, just remember that you are B.A.D. 5. When health challenges seem to overtake your body, just remember that you are B.A.D. 6. When the spirit of depression tries to overtake your mind, just remember that you are B.A.D. 7. When you have more month than money, just remember that you are B.A.D. 8. When your mode of transportation is not working right, just remember that you are B.A.D. 9. When the spirit of grief tries to paralyze you, just remember that you are B.A.D. 10. And when you wake in the morning to a brand new day, just shout to the heavens, Hallelujah!

Testimonies

In this part of the book, I allowed some true believers to give a testimony of their faith.

S.K. Edwards

WHY I PRAISE & ARE THANKFUL....

ABOUT 7-8 YEARS AGO I WAS LEFT FOR DEAD... LYNCHED(jumped) BY 7 PPL THAT BROKE RIBS & BROKE MY SKULL IN 3 PLACES (TRIPOD FRACTURE) & BROKE THE BONE CONNECTED TO MY LEFT EYE SOCKET, ALONG WITH SEVERAL INJURIES.... I WAS TOLD I HAD INJURIES TO MY BRAIN & I COULD LOOSE SIGHT IN MY LEFT EYE... HAD SURGERY & MY WHOLE LEFT SIDE ON MY FACE IS HELD TOGETHER BY "PLATES"... I REMEMBER THE DOCTOR SAYIN I STILL COULD GO BLIND & THE INJURIES TO MY BRAIN COULD MOUNT TO MEMORY LOST & FUCTION OF SUM OF BODY OPERATION OF MOVING MY ARMS & LEGS & MOTOR SKILLS... REHAB WAS SAID COULD TAKE MONTHS OR YEARS ... I REMEMBER A NURSE COMIN TO MY BEDSIDE AND HOLDING MY HAND AND "PRAYING" OVER ME... I REPEATED WHAT I COULD OF THE PRAYER WHILE I WAS ALONE & CONSTANTLY PRAYING OVER MYSELF... AND IN WHAT SHOULD HAVE TOOK MONTHS OF

His Grace & Mercy

ME REHABING, I WAS UP & ABOUT WITH "NO" SHOWING OF ANY MAJOR DAMAGE TO MY BRAIN & RESTORED EYE SIGHT WITHIN 3 WEEKS !!!!!!! GO BY THAT I DONT TELL MY "LORD & SAVIOR" THANK YOU!!!!! LIFE ITSELF IS A BLESSING !!!! NEVER TAKE IT FOR GRANTED!!!!
NOW OFF TO CHURCH I GO THE DOCTORS SAID ON MY MONTHLY CHECK UPS THAT I HEALED FASTER THAN HE EVER SEEN & THAT I MUST HAVE "GREAT GENETICS"...
I REPLIED "NO I HAVE A "GREAT GOD" !!!! THERE NOT A DAY THAT!!!! PRAISE HIM WITH MY ALL !!!!!
GOD BLESS YOU ALL THAT TOOK TIME TO READ ONE OF MY "TESTIMONIES"..

Nyce

People don't know when God puts you in place where there's no turning back...there's actually no turning back. I'd been asking God to reveal some things to me and of course you know if you ask God

S.K. Edwards

he'll show you. Trust me he did. When God take's you out of a situation its not mindful to put yourself back in it. When God say's go you better go or suffer the consequences. One thing I've learned is God doesnt lie. We look at our situations as the worst thing in the world but God looks at it as a lesson. I've never been so close to God than I have these last 3 years. Never love anybody more than you love yourself other than God. God has a way of bringing out the worst in a person so you can see the best in yourself. Everything last for a season when your time is up you gotta go. We go through in order to get through to the next level.

Rachael Jacob Powers

In 2009, I was diagnosed with a blood disease called Myelofibrosis. It gave me seven years to live and the cure had to be done before I was 43 and I was 41. Because I have no full siblings the cure was a50/50 chance of killing me. After two years of testing and 3 months of blood transfusions

His Grace & Mercy

another bone marrow biopsy was ordered for me. The Sunday before the testing was to be done there was a lot of prayer for me at the church and healing bestowed upon me which I accepted in my heart. The test was done on that Monday. It took a few days for the doctors to read the results the same doctor that diagnosed me was the same doctor that read the results again. He called all of his co-workers in the office and set my results and X-rays down on the table and ask what was different without letting anybody know who the patient was and they all agreed that the older one was a person with Myelofibrosis and the other one was a regular patient. When he told them that they were the same patient they were all in shock. You see Myelofibrosis does not cure itself it turns into Leukemia and then you die. BUT my GOD is AWESOME! He used this as a testimony of how wonderful He is. It has been three years since the first diagnosis and one year since the final. I have not had a blood transfusion since April 2011, Have gained 65 pounds (I was -100). Got my hair back and all. My God is awesome and His Word never fails.

Antoinette Lee

Know when you've been blessed by God!

When all else fails in this life, we have a higher power; I found out through life's lessons, worries, trials and tribulations- where all of my help came from!

I praise my Heavenly Father for His written word that saved a wretch like me.

I thank Him for His precious Son Jesus Christ whom paid the awesome price for my redemption, healing, prosperity, salvation, deliverance and life itself.

His Grace & Mercy

I can go on and on about The Lord's grace and tender mercies toward me and my family.

Many of my friends and their families have been blessed tremendously by The Lord.

I personally knew a man whom in his childhood, through his teen years, to adulthood suffered with intestinal issues.

Basically all of this man's life he suffered with breathing, bronchial problems. Eventually, doctor's had to perform surgery on this man. Leaving him to live his life with a half lung. Not many survive long on only a half lung! This dynamo-of-a-man did live successfully until the age of 49 and a half years. People prayed continually for this man's healing and the effectual prayer of the righteous availed much! The doctor's said he would live to the age of 50 in his condition. The Lord spared this dynamo-of-a-man to live successfully until the age of 49 and a half years old. It was not so much of what the earth-doctor's said, it was what Dr. Jesus proclaimed! This man lived a life filled with a joyful spirit, his smile encouraged others to take -the-chip- off

S.K. Edwards

their shoulder's and this man was never swayed by dismay. I was so proud of this certain man. He was an artist by nature, drawing and painting art of any object from thought. A singer in his own right, simply an amazing hard-act-to-follow.

This man in whom I reference was and remains my older biological brother whom we all loved and admired.

His name, *Melvin Phillip Norman..........................*

Remembering,

A Legend & Legacy!!!!!!

Vernetta Norman

I am a very ambitious young lady was born with Cerebral Palsy is a neurological condition that affects the cerebral cortex of

His Grace & Mercy

the brain . As a result of my cerebral I am unable to walk on my own. However, I use a wheelchair which aids me getting where I want to go. I weighted only one pound and a half a birth. According to doctors I wasn't suppose to live pass the first few of birth. God is the ultimate doctors he had and still have plans for me. Although I attended a special school for twenty years, I was mainstreamed at the age of twelve and went on to achieve beyond my teachers expectations. I graduated in the top ten of my high school class , ranking number six of 147 students. I also hold two college degrees from J Sargeant Reynolds & Virginia Commonwealth University with a Bachelors in Interdisciplinary Studies. God has blessed me with the spoon to stir gift writing poetry. I have two poetry books on Amazon. I give JESUS CHRIST the credit for all my success though him all things are possible! I truly see my disability as blessing not a burden. I hope that people will learn something from reading my testimony. I hope they understand that regardless of my

S.K. Edwards

physical I do enjoy life to the fullest. I try to live one day and prayer at a time! doing what I can when I can the best can. I'm not perfect, so when I fail it just gives me a chance to everything people think I can't do even better. I love GOD for seeing me through! The journey its over so all those who enjoy watching me. I know I'm special. Enjoy the show. Let the church say a resounding AMEN!

Terika McQuinn

I'm a believer that I can do all things through Christ who strengthens me. I know that there's a "Mighty God" we serve, when no one else can see he always manages to see "The Best in Me". His grace and miraculous powers always have me confessing "You're an awesome God". "There's no weapon" formed against me that shall prosper, his "Amazing graces" keeps "Shifting the atmosphere" … Trails and Tribulations are inevitable to miss, but when I endure pain I know joy will come in the morning. The rain will come but "I told

His Grace & Mercy

the Storm" to pass, because even through my hurt "I Smile". Being a witness to a mother battling this epidemic we call Cancer and defeating it all by his will lets me know that "He has he hands on you", we must keep in mind that these battles that comes forth aren't ours, "The battle is the Lord's". My struggles are my motivation and my motivation is increased when I think of his goodness and all he gives to me, my soul cries out, my burdens become light as feathers, my determination to not fail becomes increased, my faith grows abundantly and hopes that I make it to heaven with a job "Well done". If I had a million tongues it still wouldn't be enough to confess there's "Nobody Greater" him. He will never leave me nor forsake me, he wouldn't never put on me "More than I can bear," I can "Testify" that forever and always "I need your glory". My testimony is that "I've never seen the righteous forsaken" no desires for "Silver and Gold," "I rather have Jesus". I'm "Glad I've got Jesus." My prayers allow me to stand tall

S.K. Edwards

and "Stomp" on my doubters, evil doers and non believers. When I'm feeling down I remember he says "Be encouraged" no matter what's going on, "Jesus is my help" and whenever I call him "He's a on time God" and he "Speaks to my heart". I promise to take my stress and "Leave it at the alter," I will praise dance and raise my hands "In the Sanctuary," with my obedience "God's has a blessing" with my name on it. "Praise is what I'll do" and, "I'll trust you Lord" because no matter what "Jesus can work it out"... This is my "TESTIMONY"

LaShell Taylor

His Grace & Mercy

Calendar Quotes

S.K. Edwards

January: Pay attention; I am going to reveal the truth of every situation and uncover manipulations and deceptions that have hindered your progression in fulfilling My purposes, says the Lord. It is time for you to see clearly and to be free from delusions and fantasies. The more clearly you see and understand truth, the greater your freedom and empowerment in the realm of the Spirit. It is your destiny to be free.
John 8:32 "And you shall know the truth, and the truth shall make you free."

His Grace & Mercy

February: Be patient and wait

for the proper time and opportunity to deal with places of division and strife. There are corrections to be made, but certainly not in the heat of the moment. I am in process of revealing hidden motives and attitudes in yourself and others that can result in honest examination and communication. Refuse to rise up in pride in any confrontation. Humility is the key to resolution says the Lord.

Ephesians 4:31-32 Let all bitterness, wrath, anger, clamor, and evil speaking be put away from you, with all malice. [32] And be kind to one another, tenderhearted, forgiving one another, even as God in Christ forgave you.

S.K. Edwards

March: In a dream I was in my father's house. My parents were gone, but they had both a shower and a bathtub, and some people from our church came into the house to get cleaned up for the church service. When I awoke, I knew that there had been twelve people who had gotten cleaned up. Twelve is enough, the number symbolizing divine government, signifying that God is in charge. And, the Lord said that He wants to manifest His presence among His people in a fresh way, but we have to clean ourselves up spiritually to prepare a place for Him to do His work.

Psalms 119:9 How can a young man cleanse his way? By taking heed according to Your word.

His Grace & Mercy

April: Watch for ways that small adjustments can make a difference in the outcome you desire. It won't be difficult, but will require that you pay attention and be diligent to do what is necessary to achieve your goal. As you do that in the natural realm, you can also apply this principle to the spiritual realm. You must maintain your eternal perspective in everything, says the Lord...

2 Corinthians 4:17-18 watch for our light affliction, which is but for a moment, is working for us a far more exceeding and eternal weight of glory, while we do not look at the things which are seen, but at the things which are not seen. For the things which are seen are temporary, but the things which are not seen are eternal.

S.K. Edwards

May: Raise up a standard of faith in the midst of your circumstances. Take every opportunity to trust Me with all of your heart. Refuse to allow negativity, doubt, or unbelief to undermine your rock-solid faith, says the Lord. Face your fears and overcome. The outcome of your situation depends on it! Be strong and resilient even in great difficulty. I am with you to bring you through to victory.

Hebrews 10:23 Let us hold fast the confession of our hope without wavering, for He who promised is faithful.

His Grace & Mercy

June: I am releasing a wave of extraordinary grace that will see you through the weeks ahead. For, I will indeed empower you to do what is necessary to fulfill that which is required of you. This is a time to lean on Me for strength and wisdom. Do not forget that I am your help in times of trouble, so you must not depend on your own understanding. Rather, rise up in the supernatural realm of the Spirit to gain insight and spiritual support, says the Lord.

2 Corinthians 12:9 And He said to me, "My grace is sufficient for you, for my strength is made perfect in weakness." Therefore most gladly I will rather boast in my weakness, that the power of Christ may rest upon me.

S.K. Edwards

July: Guard your heart, and do not allow the systems of the world to divide your affections. Your dedication to Me and My kingdom must be as strong and sure as eternity. Temporary conditions and demands cannot take preeminence, so you have to watch for all manner of seduction that would take you away from spiritual reality, says the Lord.

Matthew 6:24 "No one can serve two masters; for either he will hate the one and love the other, or else he will be loyal to the one and despise the other. You cannot serve God and mammon."

His Grace & Mercy

August: A number of things will require and even demand your attention, but you must take things in stride and exercise great patience. Truly, I will stretch your time and give you the necessary physical, mental and emotional resources to deal with every situation if you will only put your trust in Me to do so. Frustration will not only kill faith, but will also prolong the process. Refuse to get overwhelmed, says the Lord.

Galatians 5:24-25 Now those who belong to Christ have crucified the flesh with its passions and desires. If we live by the Spirit, let us also behave in accordance with the Spirit.

S.K. Edwards

September: When you are faced with a difficult situation take the time to be quiet and ask for direction and wisdom. Your first instinct will be to move ahead without benefit of careful thought and consideration of the problem. Don't panic. Stay calm and work through your dilemma with confidence that nothing is too difficult for Me, says the Lord, and I will show you the way.

Psalm 5:8 Lead me, O LORD, in your righteousness because of my enemies; make Your way straight before my face.

His Grace & Mercy

October: Set a watch for all manner of seduction that will take you away from maintaining right relationship with Me, says the Lord. These are days when you must fight to keep spiritual focus. Be faithful and refuse to get sidetracked by the world, the flesh or the devil. The fight will be worth the victory. Stay close to Me.

1 John 2:16 For all that is in the world-the lust of the flesh, the lust of the eyes, and the pride of life-is not of the Father but is of the world.

S.K. Edwards

November: Rejoice that I am with you and among you, says the Lord. I have called you to be a light in the darkness, and you shall shine and bring My glory into every situation if you will only surrender to My leading. Do not despair when you see darkness and godlessness all around you, for I tell you honestly that the deeper and more profound the darkness, the more prevalent your light. Shine on!

Matthew 5:14-16 "You are the light of the world. A city that is set on a hill cannot be hidden. Nor do they light a lamp and put it under a basket, but on a lamp stand, and it gives light to all who are in the house. Let your light so shine before men, that they may see your good works and glorify your Father in heaven."

His Grace & Mercy

December: Your time of

transition has accelerated. You are rapidly entering a new phase where what you have counted on to be solid and stable has transcended to new heights. Just when you thought that you had reached the limit of your expectations and abilities, you will be required to go beyond what you could have ever considered or believed. Prepare to be stretched, says the Lord.

Ephesians 3:20-21 Now to Him who is able to do exceedingly abundantly above all that we ask or think, according to the power that works in us, to Him be glory in the church by Christ Jesus to all generations, forever and ever.

S.K. Edwards

His Grace & Mercy

Published through

Choice Publishing

Richmond, Va 23225

s.k.edwards.webs.com

S.K. Edwards

Also available from

Choice Publishing

LIVE! LAUGH! LOVE!

Available online

Createspace.com/3683642

Poetry at it's best

His Grace & Mercy

This book was printed in the U.S.

Made in the USA
Charleston, SC
01 February 2013